the little book of
LOVE

lucy lane

summersdale

THE LITTLE BOOK OF LOVE

Copyright © Summersdale Publishers Ltd, 2018

Text by Claire Berrisford

Heart icon © vector_ic/Shutterstock.com

An Hachette UK Company
www.hachette.co.uk

Summersdale Publishers Ltd
Part of Octopus Publishing Group Limited
Carmelite House
50 Victoria Embankment
LONDON
EC4Y 0DZ
UK

www.summersdale.com

Printed and bound in the Czech Republic

ISBN: 978-1-78685-528-2

Substantial discounts on bulk quantities of Summersdale books are available to corporations, professional associations and other organisations. For details contact general enquiries: telephone: +44 (0) 1243 771107 or email: enquiries@summersdale.com.

INTRODUCTION

When it comes to love, our actions speak louder than words. Whether you're already in a relationship and looking for ways to keep things fresh, or you're hoping for love to blossom and need some first-date ideas, this little book will help you show your special someone just how you feel. Filled with top tips for relationship success and amorous quotes to sweep your special someone off their feet, it's sure to spark romance. It won't be long before love is in the air!

I have a **strong will** to love you for **eternity**.

Milan Kundera

THERE IS NO INSTINCT LIKE THE HEART.

Lord Byron

MAKE TIME FOR THE LITTLE THINGS

Love has a reputation for being expressed in sweeping statements and grand gestures, so it makes sense to think that the more you love someone, the more you have to do to impress them. But love isn't just about doing something big – love is about all the little things too! Whether you're in a long-term relationship or just starting out, small everyday gestures can speak volumes about how you feel. Things like always remembering a goodnight kiss, asking your partner how their day went or carrying their bag for them if it's heavy – these moments are what makes your relationship what it is, because they show that you care. Of course, there's nothing wrong with pulling out all the stops every now and then, but to keep your relationship the best and strongest it can be, remember to make time for the little things, too – it will make all the difference.

WHEN YOU'RE LUCKY ENOUGH TO MEET YOUR ONE PERSON, THEN LIFE TAKES A TURN FOR THE BEST. IT CAN'T GET BETTER THAN THAT.

John Krasinski

I was, and am, swept away. I believe there are some things in life you can't deny or rationalise, and love is one of them.

Cate Blanchett

TELL THEM YOU LOVE THEM

It might seem like an obvious thing to suggest, but saying those three little words can make a world of difference! It's easy to take your own feelings for granted but everybody needs to hear that they're loved. Making sure your partner knows you love them and appreciate them is one of the best ways to keep your relationship happy and strong. Or, taking the plunge and telling your special someone just how you feel could take your relationship to the next level.

I ask you to
pass through life
at my side
– to be my
second self,
and best earthly
companion.

Charlotte Brontë

LOVE NOTES

Nothing gives you a boost like a surprise message from your special someone. Send them a text during the day and ask how they are, send a funny picture or even some heart emojis. Perhaps you could send your love the old-fashioned way and leave a little note for them to find later – pop it inside a book or slip it into their bag while they're not looking. Whether it's silly or soppy, it's always lovely to know that someone is thinking about you!

IF I WERE TO LIVE A THOUSAND YEARS, I WOULD BELONG TO YOU FOR ALL OF THEM.

Michelle Hodkin

CREATE MINI TRADITIONS

Doing small things together is a great way to create a bond between you. You could declare Thursday night a 'film night', regularly go to a particular coffee shop together, or find a favourite spot in your town or city to visit every now and then. Whatever routines you establish will become 'your thing' and will bring you closer together.

To be brave is
to love someone
unconditionally, without
expecting anything in
return. To just give.
That takes courage.

Madonna

TOP TIP: COMMUNICATION IS KEY

It might sound like old news, but the key to a happy, long-lasting relationship is communication. In a sentence: if something is bothering you, don't bottle it up inside! If it's a work issue, or a worry about a friend or family member, talking about it will help to take the burden off you, and sharing your thoughts with your partner brings you closer together. If it's a problem that you're having with your partner, then it's even more important to talk it out – if you let the issue simmer away inside, it will turn into feelings of resentment and drive you apart. It can be a difficult and uncomfortable experience, but being honest about what you're feeling is the best way to build trust and understanding between you both. Remember, though, that it works both ways – always give your partner the time and space to speak about their problems and listen to what they have to say as well.

Let your **love** be like
the **misty rains,**
coming softly, but
flooding the river.

Malagasy proverb

LOVE MUST BE AS MUCH A LIGHT, AS IT IS A FLAME.

Henry David Thoreau

OFFER COMPLIMENTS

It's always nice to be noticed, so tell your special someone what you like about them – their eyes or their smile, the way that they laugh – or compliment something that they're able to do. Perhaps they make an amazing lasagne, or they're great at picking out the right music to suit the mood, or they always know what to say to make you feel better. Whatever it is that you love about them, make sure they hear about it.

I love thee with the
breath, smiles, tears,
of all my life.

Elizabeth Barrett Browning

PACK A PICNIC

A picnic is one of life's simple pleasures and perfect for a date. Make your food before you go, rather than buying it, to add a homemade touch to your day. Pack drinks, snacks and a blanket and set aside an hour or two. Pick a scenic, open spot if you like to people-watch, or somewhere more secluded if you want to spend quiet time together, and enjoy a leisurely afternoon with each other, watching the world go by.

Lots of people want to ride with you in the **limo**, but what you want is someone who will **take the bus** with you when the limo breaks down.

Oprah Winfrey

BE AFFECTIONATE

Small gestures of affection are a great way of making your beau or belle feel loved and appreciated: if you're out together, hold hands as you walk; greet each other with a proper hug; surprise the other person with a kiss on the cheek, shoulder or forehead just because. These moments of closeness actually increase our levels of oxytocin, a hormone that helps us bond with others and feel calm – so a little bit of affection goes a long way!

**HER LIPS
ON HIS COULD
TELL HIM BETTER
THAN ALL HER
STUMBLING
WORDS.**

Margaret Mitchell

LOG OFF AND TUNE IN

When you're spending quality time together – be it talking, watching TV or having a meal – make sure your phone stays out of it. If you're continually distracted by your screen, you're not giving the other person your full attention and it sends the message that you think they're not worth your time. If you find it hard to ignore the buzz of notifications, put your phone in your bag or on a table out of temptation's reach. Don't let it become the third wheel in your relationship!

Love is the strongest
force the world
possesses.

Mahatma Gandhi

I want the
deepest, darkest...
parts of you that you
are **afraid** to share
with anyone because
I love you
that much.

Lady Gaga

LOVE IS COMPOSED OF A SINGLE SOUL INHABITING TWO BODIES.

Aristotle

TOP TIP:
BE ALL EARS

Communication might be the key piece of advice for successful relationships, but it doesn't work without the ability to listen, too. The two are connected – if one person speaks, the other must listen; it's being able to do this that builds the strong bond of trust and understanding between you both. If your partner comes to you with a problem or worry, let them talk before jumping in to say anything. When you ask how their day was, really listen to their answer. Ask them questions about the things that they've said and give them your full attention as you have your conversation. Seek them out for their advice – whether it's on your outfit for the day, or about bigger life decisions you have to deal with. This is the foundation of being open and communicative with your significant other (SO) and it will give your relationship the strong roots it needs to last.

I love you,
Not only for
what you are,
But for what I am
when I am with you.

Roy Croft

IN YOUR LIGHT
I LEARN HOW
TO LOVE.

Rumi

MARVELLOUS MUSEUMS

If you're in the mood for culture, why not visit a museum? As well as being an often low-budget (or even free) way to see something interesting and unusual, they're a great place for a first date. Even if you don't have a great interest in the exhibition itself, the museum can be a quirky backdrop for getting to know someone, or for spending some quality time with your SO. Some museums even offer special evening opening hours with drinks – an original and romantic setting for an evening for two.

Sometimes the
heart sees what
is invisible to
the eye.

H. Jackson Brown Jr

PHOTO BOOTH FUN

The best dates are those that make memories, and photos are one of the surest ways to capture moments to last for years to come – the sillier the better! Most smartphones and tablets come with a photo booth app which has various filters to distort your faces in weird and wonderful ways. The results can be hilarious, and once you've started laughing you won't be able to stop!

THERE'S NO BAD CONSEQUENCE TO LOVING FULLY, WITH ALL YOUR HEART. YOU ALWAYS GAIN BY GIVING LOVE.

Reese Witherspoon

TOP TIP: DARE TO BE DIFFERENT

Having similar interests is often said to be one of the main criteria if you want to build a happy and long-lasting relationship. It's true that liking the same things is an advantage, as it means you have common ground that links you together. A lot of couples find that they meet each other through the interests that they share, whether that's through a hobby or club, or through work. But to be a perfect match with someone doesn't mean you have to be clones of each other; a shared interest certainly isn't the only condition for a strong relationship. Do you feel comfortable with one another? Can you make each other laugh? Do you find that you think in similar ways, or reach similar conclusions? Do you want to make each other happy? These are also important factors to consider. So even if you might appear to be chalk and cheese, as long as you connect and enjoy each other's company, that's a good indicator that you're a great match.

I HAVE SOMEONE
WHO I CAN
TALK TO ABOUT
ANYTHING, AND
SOMEONE WHO
I CARE MORE
ABOUT THAN I'VE
CARED ABOUT
ANYBODY.

George Clooney

To love and be loved
is to feel the sun
from both sides.

David Viscott

TAKE A ROMANTIC ROAD TRIP

There's romance to the idea of packing your bags and exploring somewhere neither of you have ever been before – which is why a mini road trip is a perfect date idea. Use whatever transport is available to you and go on an adventure together for the day – whether it's driving down pretty country lanes, taking the train up to a big city or just riding the bus a few stops further than you'd usually go!

When I saw you I
fell in love, and
you **smiled** because
you **knew**.

Arrigo Boito

SURPRISE THEM WITH A GIFT

Everybody loves presents! So what better way to give your special someone a boost and show them they are on your mind than by giving them a gift? The best gifts are the most personal so, if you have time to spend on it, you could make something – an album of your favourite photos together or a playlist of all your favourite songs, for instance. A personal gift can also show that you listen to your partner – you could buy them a book or a CD that they've been talking about. But you don't necessarily have to spend money to make your loved one feel appreciated: perhaps you'll see something that reminds you of an in-joke you have together – take a picture of it and show it to them when you see them next. Whatever you surprise them with, they'll be happy to know that you were thinking of them.

TRUE LOVE DOESN'T COME TO YOU, IT HAS TO BE INSIDE YOU.

Julia Roberts

It's an unexplainable feeling, an expression. It's a touch, it's a feel. Once you feel it, it's like no other thing in the world.

Snoop Dogg on love

TOP TIP: BE KIND

Next to the big qualities that are important to a relationship, like honesty, respect and trust, kindness might sound like a small thing to pay attention to. But, just like other small things (like the power of those three little words…) it shouldn't be underestimated! Being kind to your SO is one of the most essential elements to a respectful and enduring relationship. It can come in many different forms, too. While kindness is sometimes about doing your share of the washing-up, it's also about not shutting your partner down immediately if they say something you disagree with. It's about choosing not to pursue an argument, diverting it if you can feel one brewing, or saying you'll discuss the issue another time. It's being able to admit when you're wrong and apologising when it's needed. Essentially, kindness is about letting go of the little things that could cause friction and putting your relationship first so that both of you can move forward together, united as a team.

May you live as long
as you wish and love
as long as you live.

Robert A. Heinlein

LOVE IS THE ONLY GOLD.

Alfred, Lord Tennyson

LEND A HAND

Doing something helpful without being asked is always a good way to gain the affections of your SO. It could be a chore, like taking out the bins, doing the food shop or taking the dog for a walk. Maybe you could run an errand for them, like posting a parcel or buying a coffee. Any small gesture to help them is sure to be noticed and appreciated.

Love takes off
the masks that we
fear we cannot live
without and know we
cannot live within.

James Baldwin

COOK UP A STORM

It's often said that the way to someone's heart is through their stomach, so why not cook your special someone their favourite meal as a treat? Even better if you can keep it as a surprise. Not only does this show that you're happy to put some effort in for them, if you know what their favourite meal is, it shows that you listen, too! Add some flowers to the table and some music to set the mood, and you're all set for a perfect evening.

REMEMBER THAT
WHEREVER YOUR
HEART IS, THERE
YOU WILL FIND
YOUR TREASURE.

Paulo Coelho

TURN RIGHT

Sometimes the best dates are the simplest, so here's a fun game to try. The rules are simple: go outside and start walking. Each time you reach a junction you can only keep going forward or turn right. It's deceptively simple – and a great way to discover something new. You may even find a hidden gem of a place right around the corner! Try the game on a bike if you want to travel further and take it to the next level.

Kiss me, and
you will see how
important I am.

Sylvia Plath

Love is the only
flower that grows and
blossoms without the
aid of the seasons.

Kahlil Gibran

MY HEART HAS MADE ITS MIND UP AND I'M AFRAID IT'S YOU.

Wendy Cope

TWITCH TO WOO

Birdwatching might not be the first thing you think of when searching for date ideas, but there's a first time for everything! Birds are among the most visible wildlife there is – and with their cheeky, inquisitive characters, perhaps they are also some of the most entertaining. You don't need any special equipment to go birdwatching – just plenty of layers if it's cold – and it gives you and your own lovebird a chance to spend some time alone together in the fresh air. Watch for birds in the scenery around you, stake out a spot by some birdfeeders (always a good place to spot them) or listen for birdsong in the trees. You could go to a park, garden or beach, or look up birdwatching hotspots or RSPB reserves near you to watch for feathered friends. As long as you're patient, they're bound to turn up.

MEET THE FAMILY

Being prepared to go to events where your partner's friends or family will be present is a great way to show that you care about them. The fact that they ask you to attend means that they want to involve you in their life and, if you accept, it shows that you want to be involved, too. Even if their friends or family aren't who you would normally choose to spend time with, the fact that you're willing to be polite and friendly will mean a lot to them.

I WANT EVERYONE TO MEET YOU. YOU'RE MY FAVOURITE PERSON OF ALL TIME.

Rainbow Rowell

TOP TIP: BE YOUR OWN PERSON

The closeness and friendship that a relationship affords is one of the best feelings you can have, and as your relationship develops you'll probably find yourself spending more and more time together – and this is certainly no bad thing! However, you may also find that you're constantly trying to think of ways to make them happy, ways to spend time with them and ways to support them – before you know it, your lives can come to revolve around each other, leaving no time for you as individuals. A healthy relationship needs balance, so retain this by keeping up with your own interests and hobbies, independently of each other. Remember to stay in touch with your friends, too, as they are there to love and support you just as much as your partner is. Everybody needs time and space to themselves, and having your own life alongside the one that you share with your SO will help your relationship to flourish.

If you can be
yourselves
around each other
100 per cent
of the time… you'll
never have a dull
moment **together**.

Will Smith

WITHOUT LOVE, THE WORLD ITSELF WOULD NOT SURVIVE.

Lope de Vega

EXPRESS YOUR LOVE

If you want to show your love for someone, why not take a more traditional route to wooing them and express your feelings through music or poetry? You don't have to be a professional to pull this off. The time and effort that's required to create something is often worth just as much – if not more – than the finished work! Your special someone is sure to be touched that you spent so much time on them.

I kissed a lot of
frogs and now I've
found my prince.

Joan Collins

SEEING STARS

Nothing says romance like gazing up at the night sky with your favourite person by your side. Wrap up warm, take a blanket (and maybe some hot chocolate!) and find a spot to admire the stars. Anywhere high up, away from light pollution, will give you the best views – although make sure wherever you're going is safe to be at night. Look into whether there are any particular stargazing sites near you before you go. The best time to go is on a cold, clear night – ideally when there isn't a full moon (as its light will wash out the sky). If you have them, binoculars can also improve your stargazing experience. And if you're not content just to gaze, there are a number of apps you can download to your smartphone to help you identify the constellations and planets.

YOURS IS
THE LIGHT
BY WHICH MY
SPIRIT'S BORN:
YOU ARE MY
SUN, MY MOON,
AND ALL MY
STARS.

E. E. Cummings

Love does not consist in gazing at each other but in looking outward together in the same direction.

Antoine de Saint-Exupéry

TASTY DATE

Liven up a dinner date by making the dinner yourself! Pizza is a great meal to make as a pair – have fun taking turns to knead the dough, and experiment with different toppings until you find the perfect combination. If you want to be adventurous, try cooking a dish or cuisine that neither of you have cooked before. Eat your homemade dinner by candlelight and you've got the perfect recipe for a romantic date.

In dreams and in
love there are no
impossibilities.

János Arany

MAKE TIME FOR THE ONE YOU LOVE

Your partner is one of the most important people in your life – so make sure they know it! If you have a date planned with them, make sure you keep it. If an event you're considering clashes with something your partner would like to do, consider cancelling or postponing your event in order to spend more time with them. And, even though we all have busy calendars, be sure to check in with your SO about when you have things scheduled, or let them know about what you're planning before you agree to things.

Rather than being an invasion of privacy, extending this courtesy means that you're both on the same page. All these small things show that you're willing to make time for your partner.

GET CREATIVE

Working on a creative project together is a great way to strengthen the bond between you and enjoy some quality time together. You could try making photo frames or putting together an album of your favourite snaps, playing or writing music together, painting something to hang on the wall, making Christmas decorations, or even shooting a film using your smartphone or a cheap camera – the possibilities are endless!

LOVE IS A GAME THAT TWO CAN PLAY AND BOTH WIN.

Eva Gabor

VOUCHER DATE

Take a step out of your comfort zone and dare to do something different for this date idea! Search online for vouchers that are valid in your area and take your date somewhere unusual. There could be any number of things available to you – from falconry experiences to photography courses, to race-car driving, to adventure park discounts. You'll be able to do something wacky that you might never normally have thought of – and make some great memories together in the process.

Love shall be our token;
love be yours and
love be mine.

Christina Rossetti

LOVE HAS NO
UTTERMOST, AS
THE STARS HAVE
NO NUMBER
AND THE SEA
NO REST.

Eleanor Farjeon

Love conquers
all things.

Virgil

TOP TIP: APPRECIATE YOUR PARTNER

If you've been in a relationship for a while, it's easy to fall into familiar patterns. This isn't necessarily a bad thing – it's great to feel comfortable with someone, to know what to expect from them and to be able to rely on them. But when you get to this stage, it's also important not to take them for granted. All it takes is a few simple gestures every now and then to make your partner feel loved and appreciated: thank them when they do things for you; compliment them;

ask them questions about their day; offer to help them out; encourage them when they are unsure; and tell them that you love them! However you choose to express it, whether it's through the things you say or the things you do, make sure that your partner feels special and knows they matter to you; this helps both of you to feel happy and secure.

They say love is the
best investment;
the more you give,
the **more you
get** in return.

Audrey Hepburn

MY VERY SOUL DEMANDS YOU.

Charlotte Brontë

DRESS UP

Getting dressed up to the nines makes any night feel special – combine that with a date night and it's a sure-fire way to get the sparks flying. You could splash out on a fancy restaurant meal if your budget allows, but a glitzy evening doesn't have to have a venue to match. Choose anywhere you like to show off your finery, such as a bar or a local music event. You don't even have to leave the house – why not enjoy a glamorous *soirée* for two in the comfort of your own home?

Lovers alone wear
sunlight.

E. E. Cummings

BE A CHEERLEADER

One of the best ways to build a bond is to make sure your special someone feels supported, and a great way to do this is to celebrate their successes. Whether they've made progress with a personal project, achieved something at work or in class, or ventured outside their comfort zone, make sure you focus on them and give them the praise and support that they deserve – perhaps you could celebrate the occasion with a lunch date, a small gift or even some bubbly!

When I feel the support that I have from him, I feel invincible. There's someone behind you on your good days, and someone in front of you on your bad days.

Emily Blunt on her husband

SLEEP UNDER THE STARS

Get in touch with your wild side and go camping with your sweetheart! It has all the fun of a weekend trip, without the price-tag of staying in a city, so it suits all budgets – plus the short break from technology and the conveniences of modern-day life mean it's a great way to truly spend time with each other. Plus, what could be more romantic than a campfire? Investigate whether there are any campsites in your area and what kind of facilities they offer. You could take your own tent, although some sites offer pre-pitched tents if you don't have one of your own. Take plenty of layers, some comfy cushions and blankets to snuggle up with – and don't forget the marshmallows! If full-on camping isn't for you, why not try glamping? You can experience sleeping under the stars in a tent without having to forego the conveniences of running water, electricity and a comfy bed!

LOVE IS ALWAYS BEFORE YOU.

André Breton

Love is something
eternal; the aspect
may change, but
not the essence.

Vincent van Gogh

TEACH EACH OTHER SOMETHING

Even if you have shared interests, there will inevitably be things you can do that your date can't – and vice versa! Break down the barriers between you by teaching each other something new. Whether it's learning an instrument or a type of dance, playing a sport, speaking a language or discovering a craft like sewing or making pottery – share your skills with your date and you share your world with them.

THERE ARE ALL KINDS OF LOVE IN THIS WORLD BUT NEVER THE SAME LOVE TWICE.

F. Scott Fitzgerald

TOP TIP:
SPEAK KINDLY

You're out with a group of friends for the evening and the conversation turns to your beau or belle – what would you say about yours? Is your first instinct to offer up a story of how they've annoyed you recently or how much they get on your nerves? Or is it about something kind they did for you, or something funny that happened to you both? The way that you talk about your SO to others reveals more than you might think about your relationship – it could even reveal feelings that you didn't know you had. If your instinct is to talk them down, then it may be that you need to take a step back and ask yourself a few questions about what your relationship truly means to you. However, if your immediate thoughts about them are positive, it shows that you're in a good place with each other and that you want, first and foremost, to support them.

[She] is my foundation...
the rock, that is
the foundation
of our family, and
therefore my life.

Hugh Jackman on his wife

YOU SHOULD BE KISSED AND OFTEN, AND BY SOMEONE WHO KNOWS HOW.

Margaret Mitchell

SING KARAOKE

Try out a karaoke night at a local pub or bar and get in touch with your inner pop star. It doesn't matter if you're a singer or not – any nerves will soon vanish once you're into the swing of it – and don't forget that the silliness is all part of the fun! If you'd rather not unleash your musical 'talents' upon the world, you could always hold your singing session in the comfort of your own home; there are plenty of karaoke videos to follow online.

True love is singing
karaoke 'Under Pressure'
and letting the other
person sing the Freddie
Mercury part.

Mindy Kaling

BREAKFAST IN BED

It doesn't have to be a birthday or a special occasion to surprise your other half with breakfast in bed! Serve them their usual bowl of cereal in comfort or splash out and make them something fancier – scrambled eggs, avocado on toast, pancakes and syrup, or even a cooked breakfast. Whatever you make, you'll put a smile on their face and give them a great start to their day.

The kiss itself is **immortal**. It travels from **lip to lip**, century to century, from **age to age**.

Guy de Maupassant

TRUE LOVE CANNOT BE FOUND WHERE IT DOES NOT EXIST; NOR CAN IT BE DENIED WHERE IT DOES.

Torquato Tasso

When I think about
what makes my life
my life, and makes
sense... it's him.

Julia Roberts on her husband

THE SHOPPING GAME

This is shopping but with a twist, and a date idea with laughs guaranteed. The game is simple: pick any clothes shop and choose an outfit... for the other person! The clothes you pick are completely up to you – choose something you think your date would love, or find something they've never tried before. The only rule is that they have to try on whatever you give them and either give you a changing-room runway show or take a photo of the ensemble. Be cruel or kind... it's your choice!

LOVE IS NOT CONSOLATION. IT IS LIGHT.

Simone Weil

LEARN TO DANCE

Trying out something new is always a fun theme for a date, and learning to dance is a handy skill to have up your sleeve! Look up dance classes in your area to find something you fancy: Latin, ballroom or swing dancing are often good for couples. Or you could try salsa, ballet, jazz, contemporary, Bollywood, flamenco, tap, commercial dancing or line dancing – to name but a few! Dancing has the added bonus of keeping you fit and healthy, so it's quality time spent in more ways than one.

I look at him
every day and
he **inspires** me.

Cameron Diaz on her husband

VOLUNTEER TOGETHER

Volunteering is one of the most rewarding ways you can spend your time, and even more so when you can do it with the people you care about. Not only is it good for the community, but working towards a shared goal is a great way to bond. The possibilities are endless, so there really is something to suit everyone: walking dogs, volunteering at a soup kitchen, spending time with the elderly, tutoring students, stewarding at public events like races or open days, working with children, volunteering as a driver, coaching sports and organising charity events are just some of the ways that you can get involved. Search for opportunities in your local area and you're bound to find something that you and your special someone will be able to take part in together.

PLAY TRUTH OR DARE

If you want to really get to know your date, a game of truth or dare is the way to go. It's simple to play: choose truth and you must answer any question of your partner's choosing (for example, What's the most embarrassing thing you've been caught doing? What's the biggest lie you've ever told?); choose dare, and you must do anything your partner says (for example, talk in an accent for the next 30 minutes or do a striptease). With this game you can be as naughty as you like, so things could get a little saucy!

A kiss on the beach
when there is a full
moon is the closest
thing to heaven.

H. Jackson Brown Jr

TOP TIP: WORK OUT THE 'WHY'

Disagreements and arguments are an inevitable part of any relationship, but whether they drive you apart or bring you closer together is all down to how you handle them. If you're leaving the argument with no understanding of why your partner is acting the way that they are, you'll probably continue to feel angry and bitter. However, if you're able to work out why your partner is upset, or what's driving them to say the things that they are, then you're much closer to finding a way to resolve your differences – you can choose to clear up a misunderstanding, or 'agree to disagree' and find a middle ground where you are both happy. If you are able to do this, you will be able to grow from your arguments and understand each other better. It's widely believed that couples who are able to argue are closer and stronger – so arguing can actually be healthy for your relationship!

YOU ARE MY HEART, MY LIFE, MY ONE AND ONLY THOUGHT.

Arthur Conan Doyle

I love you
without knowing
how, or **when,**
or from **where.**

Pablo Neruda

BE A TOURIST

It's easy to overlook the amazing things on your doorstep because they're the familiar parts of everyday life, so take your date and be a tourist in your own town for the day! Visit all the highlights, take a tour bus, grab a bite at your favourite cafe or pub, and remember to take plenty of cheesy photos along the way to remember your day by. You might be surprised by the treasures that your town or city has to offer!

I am in love – and, my God, it's the greatest thing that can happen to a man.

D. H. Lawrence

MAKE A BLANKET FORT

If there's a more romantic place to chill out than a blanket fort, we are yet to discover it. All you need are sheets and blankets, something soft to snuggle up on, such as pillows or sofa cushions, some furniture and some pegs. Begin by laying down your cushions and pillows where you'd like to sit. Then gather chairs and other pieces of furniture around where you've placed your cushions and drape the blankets and sheets over the top of them to make a shelter. Use the pegs to secure your blankets in place. You may want to use items such as an umbrella or a broomstick to give the roof some extra support. For some finishing touches, add some fairy lights inside the fort for romantic mood lighting and voila – you've built the perfect hideout for movie marathons and cosy evenings together.

I know of only
one duty, and
that is to love.

Albert Camus

COME LIVE IN MY HEART AND PAY NO RENT.

Samuel Lover

APPRECIATE EACH OTHER

There's a lot of talk about how communication is the key to all good relationships, and it often seems to revolve around the idea of discussing the big issues and problems of the day. But, like anything, the little moments count just as much as the bigger ones. There are plenty of small opportunities to connect with each other throughout the day. Say good morning and goodnight, whether it's through text messages or in person. Thank your partner when they do things for you, like opening the door, carrying a bag or serving dinner. Greet them when you see them, and give them a kiss and a proper hug when you part. Ask if there's anything you can do to help – even if there's not, they will be happy to have been asked. Not only do all these things give you both a lift, but they add up: they say to your partner that you're looking out for them and that you'll always be there.

PASSION MAKES THE WORLD GO ROUND. LOVE JUST MAKES IT A SAFER PLACE.

Ice-T

Whatever our souls
are made of, his and
mine are the same.

Emily Brontë

BAKE TOGETHER

If you're in the market for a delicious date idea then why not try turning your hand to baking? Making something sweet with your sweetheart is a fun way to spend an afternoon, plus with plenty of yummy ingredients to taste test throughout the process, it's the perfect excuse to get a little flirty with each other! Be it cakes, biscuits or pastries, choose your recipe, fire up your favourite playlist and enjoy making a mess (and hopefully something delicious, too).

Everything in our
life should be
based on **love**.

Ray Bradbury

GO ON A WALK OR A HIKE

A sunny day is a perfect opportunity to go on a walk or a hike with your loved one. Not only is walking a simple and budget-friendly way to spend quality time together, but you will get to experience some stunning views of the natural world. Before setting off, make sure you choose the right trail for your ability – for instance, a steep 15-kilometre hike through rocky terrain is probably not the best choice for a beginner! Check the weather before you go, as walking in bad conditions is dangerous and, as a precaution, always let someone else know where you are going. Pack a map, suncream, an extra jumper, plenty of water and snacks, a phone and, most importantly, make sure you have sturdy footwear. Completing a walk or a hike can be incredibly rewarding (especially if there's a pub lunch at the end of it!) and if you challenge yourselves you'll have the added bonus of having pulled through and achieved something together. This shared success will only bring you closer.

It was not my
lips you kissed,
but my soul.

Judy Garland

THE WORLD NEEDS MORE LOVE AT FIRST SIGHT.

Maggie Stiefvater

TOP TIP: RESPECT PRIVACY

Your partner is out of the room for a few minutes; their phone is on the table. You also know their passcode. So what do you do? The answer? Leave the phone alone! It doesn't take a genius to know that if you're tempted to read through your partner's emails and texts, you have a slight issue with trust. Snooping through their phone will never bring you anything good: find something you don't like and you either have to bring it to light or carry that secret with you – neither of which are great outcomes. If you don't find anything incriminating, you're left with the burden of knowing that you didn't trust them, meaning that you're now the untrustworthy party. Again: not the best result. If you do get the urge to check through texts and emails, talk over your worries with your partner and get to the bottom of them. Only then will you be able to put any issues to rest and move on together.

Love should be a **tree**
whose **roots** are
deep in the earth, but
whose **branches**
extend into heaven.

Bertrand Russell

LOVE IS WHEN YOU MEET SOMEONE WHO TELLS YOU SOMETHING NEW ABOUT YOURSELF.

André Breton

SECRET DATE

Invite your beloved out on a date, but don't tell them what it is. Brief them on anything they need to wear or bring with them, but keep the details secret for as long as you can. You could take a day trip, organise tickets to see their favourite band, or even do something major like plan a holiday! Or you could keep it simple: book a restaurant and keep it secret until you arrive, for instance. Adding a little mystery will intrigue your date and make your event that little bit more special.

She is the heart
that strikes a whole
octave. After her all
songs are possible.

Rainer Maria Rilke

SPA DATE

If you've got room in your budget and you want to treat yourself and your date, why not spend an afternoon (or even a whole day) at your local spa? Not only do you both get to take a break from the rush of daily life with people who know exactly how to make you feel relaxed, but it's one of the most intimate ways you can spend a day. With all that pampering, you'll definitely be in their good books!

TO LOVE IS TO WILL THE GOOD OF THE OTHER.

Thomas Aquinas

TOP TIP: MEET IN THE MIDDLE

Compromising is never something we really want to do, but it's another one of those things that's inevitable in all relationships at some point or another. And, although it's hard to admit, sometimes the easiest way through a problem is to meet in the middle. What matters is that both of you are willing to compromise – it only works if you're both trying to find a balance to keep each other happy. If you're still not convinced, remember also that compromise doesn't have to be thought of in terms of sacrifice.

Instead, approach it as a negotiation; for instance, 'I will do X if you can do Y'. However, although it's important, compromise isn't always the answer, and sometimes it's necessary to stand up for what you want; if this is the case then don't be afraid to speak up. As long as you know when to concede and when to stand your ground, you're on the road to relationship success.

YOU KNOW IT'S
LOVE WHEN ALL
YOU WANT IS
THAT PERSON
TO BE HAPPY.

Julia Roberts

Love is the
river of life
in the world.

Henry Ward Beecher

GET YOUR SKATES ON!

For a classic date – or perhaps a nostalgic one – visit a roller skating arena or an ice rink with your date. It doesn't matter if you're not a pro as half the fun is in wobbling around the arena (and holding onto each other tightly, of course!). Laughter and fun are guaranteed, and the best thing is that it won't break the bank.

I like to believe that love
is a reciprocal thing,
that it can't really be
felt, truly, by one.

Sean Penn

When you find that one that's right for you, you feel like they were put there for you, you never want to be apart.

Joe Manganiello

THE ESKIMOS HAD FIFTY-TWO NAMES FOR SNOW BECAUSE IT WAS IMPORTANT TO THEM: THERE OUGHT TO BE AS MANY FOR LOVE.

Margaret Atwood

IT'S A DATE!

Make dates with your favourite person a part of your weekly routine – and why not try taking it in turns to decide where to go? You could meet up at lunchtimes for a stroll, a chat or a bite to eat, go for breakfast together or spend an evening with each other. Whether you're just starting out, or settled in your relationship, dating regularly keeps the flame of love alive!

The greatest healing therapy is **friendship** and **love**.

Hubert Humphrey

WORK OUT TOGETHER

If you're looking for more ways to spend time with your one and only, why not coordinate your workouts? You could meet up for a run, go for a session at the gym, or take a fitness class together. It might not be the most conventional setting for a date but working out side by side you will be able to encourage, challenge and push each other, plus you'll share a great sense of achievement – nothing can bring you closer!

THE MADNESS
OF LOVE IS
THE GREATEST
OF HEAVEN'S
BLESSINGS.

Plato

TOP TIP: KEEPING IT FRESH

Getting stuck in a rut is something that most of us dread – once you're comfortable with each other, it can feel that your time together just doesn't have that same spark that it once did. A great way to keep your relationship exciting and fresh is to try something new together. Whether it's a hobby or a sport, taking a class or travelling somewhere you've never been, doing something together for the first time will strengthen your bond, as well as giving you the excitement of something fresh! However, just because you've found a routine it doesn't mean that your relationship is in trouble, or that your feelings for one another have dimmed. All relationships ebb and flow, and it's natural to settle down into a pattern that you're both comfortable with. As long as you are able to remain open and enjoy each other's company, you're sure to have many happy years together.

Grow old along
with me! The best
is yet to be.

Robert Browning

IN LOVE,
ONE AND ONE
ARE ONE.

Jean-Paul Sartre

If you're interested in finding out
more about our books, find us on
Facebook at **Summersdale Publishers**
and follow us on Twitter
at @Summersdale.

www.summersdale.com